YOU CAN'T MAKE ME!

LEARNING ABOUT RESPECT

Katherine Eason

FOX EYE
PUBLISHING

When Mum asked Lucy to tidy up, Lucy often didn't want to.

Lucy told Mum that she couldn't make her! Lucy didn't show **RESPECT**.

When Mum made the breakfast, she asked Lucy to say **THANK YOU**.

Lucy said Mum couldn't make her!
She didn't show **RESPECT**.

When Dad walked Lucy to school, Lucy asked him to carry her bag. She should have said **PLEASE**.

But Lucy didn't want to.
She didn't show **RESPECT**.

At the end of the reading lesson, Mr Reed asked Lucy to put the books back.

Lucy said she didn't want to!
She didn't show **RESPECT**.

At break time, Lucy scratched Tilly's scooter. Tilly was **UPSET**.

But Lucy didn't care. She didn't say sorry. She didn't show **RESPECT**.

At home time, Granny asked Lucy to hold her hand. But Lucy ran ahead.

Lucy knew Granny couldn't make her. Lucy didn't show **RESPECT**.

At home, Granny asked Lucy how she would feel if no one said **PLEASE** or **THANK YOU** to her. How would she feel if someone broke her toy and didn't say sorry?

Lucy thought about how it would feel. It **DIDN'T FEEL GOOD**. Perhaps being respectful wasn't so **SILLY** after all.

The next day, Lucy tidied her room. When Mum made the breakfast, Lucy said **THANK YOU**. Loud and clear.

Granny **WINKED** at Mum.
Lucy had learnt to
show **RESPECT**!

Words and Behaviour

Lucy didn't show respect in this story and that caused a lot of problems.

There are a lot of words to do with respect in this book. Can you remember all of them?

THANK YOU

PLEASE

Let's talk about feelings and manners

This series helps children to understand difficult emotions and behaviours and how to manage them. The characters in the series have been created to show emotions and behaviours that are often seen in young children, and which can be difficult to manage.

You Can't Make Me!

The story in this book examines the reasons for showing respect. It looks at why being respectful is important and how showing respect stops others from becoming upset.

How to use this book

You can read this book with one child or a group of children. The book can be used to begin a discussion around complex behaviour such as learning to show respect.

The book is also a reading aid, with enlarged and repeated words to help children to develop their reading skills.

How to read the story

Before beginning the story, ensure that the children you are reading to are relaxed and focused.

Take time to look at the enlarged words and the illustrations, and discuss what this book might be about before reading the story.

New words can be tricky for young children to approach. Sounding them out first, slowly and repeatedly, can help children to learn the words and become familiar with them.

How to discuss the story

When you have finished reading the story, use these questions and discussion points to examine the theme of the story with children and explore the emotions and behaviour within it:

- What do you think the story was about?
- Have you been in a situation in which you didn't show respect? What was that situation?
- Do you think showing respect is silly? Why?
- Do you think being respectful is important? Why?
- What could go wrong if you are not respectful?

Titles in the series

First published in 2023 by Fox Eye Publishing
Unit 31, Vulcan House Business Centre,
Vulcan Road, Leicester, LE5 3FF
www.foxeyepublishing.com

Author: Jasmine Brooke
Art director: Paul Phillips
Cover designer: Emma Bailey
Editor: Jenny Rush

All illustrations by Novel

ISBN 978-1-80445-159-5

Printed in China